Dream Big Plan Smart
A Guide to Planning Your Dream Wedding

Narketta M. Sparkman, M.A.

"Your wedding can be everything you dream it to be, but it takes smart planning to make your dream a reality"

authorHOUSE®

AuthorHouse™
1663 Liberty Drive, Suite 200
Bloomington, IN 47403
www.authorhouse.com
Phone: 1-800-839-8640

First published by AuthorHouse   9/20/2007

ISBN: 978-1-4343-1353-9 (sc)

Printed in the United States of America
Bloomington, Indiana

This book is printed on acid-free paper.

In Loving Memory of My Grandmother

Beatrice Martin

My Inspiration

Acknowledgements

Mr. Julius Sparkman, My dear husband for all your support.

Julian, Cheyanne, and Julius, My children for keeping me focused.

Danielle Garrett for Editing and Advisement.

Wallace M. Chrouch Photography
Backcover Photograph

Photography by Lisa
Front Cover Photograph

Content

Introduction 1

Chapter One: Budget Planning 3

Chapter Two: Insuring your Special Day 7

Chapter Three: Why Hire a Wedding Consultant? 9

Chapter Four: The Ceremony 15

Chapter Five: The Reception 19

Chapter Six: Choosing Your Wedding Cake 31

Chapter Seven: Choosing Your Bridal Party 35

Chapter Eight: Bridal Attire 41

Chapter Nine: Choosing a Photographer 49

Chapter Ten: Choosing Your Video Professional 53

Chapter Eleven: Stationery 57

Chapter Twelve Wedding Décor 61

Chapter Thirteen: Entertainment 77

Chapter Fourteen: Rehearsal 81

Chapter Fifthteen: Transportation 85

Chapter Sixteen: Reserving Your Honeymoon 87

Chapter Seventeen: Your Wedding Day 90

Chapter Eighteen: Conclusion 93

Introduction

Planning a wedding can be a daunting task if you don't know where to begin. <u>Dream Big Plan Smart</u> assists you in planning your special day flawlessly, complete with guides and tips to keep you on the path to success. Each chapter is designed to guide you effortlessly through the planning process and then onto your magnificent wedding.

Before you begin, think about what you want you're wedding to be. Write down words to describe your vision. As you peruse through this guide keep your vision in mind. Your vision will assist you in making important decisions along the way.

My Vision

```



```

Chapter One:
Budget Planning

Before you begin planning your special day you must first plan a budget. Budgeting is significant to the overall outcome of your wedding. The average United States wedding according to CNN Money is $27,327 (2005). With this in mind it is important to plan accordingly. You can have a nice wedding on a small or large budget but this figure gives you an average. It also assists you in planning a realistic budget for your dream wedding. The Internet is a great resource to finding wedding statistics for your area. There are websites that allow you to find out the cost of wedding services in your area. These sites can help you project costs of services in your budget.

In the following pages you will find a budget guide that will assist you in planning a budget for the big day. You will have to project the cost for each item and tally it at the end for a final budget projection. With this total you can begin planning you dream wedding.

Tip: In order to stick to your budget you must negotiate with vendors to obtain the services you want with out going over budget.

Budget

Expense Category	Budget	Actual	Deposit
Bridal Consultant			
Ceremony			
Reception			
Photographer			
Video professional			
Florist			
Décor			
Linen			
Invitations			
Transportation			
Insurance			
Attendant Gifts			
Favors			
Hotel			
Honeymoon			
Attire			
Bridesmaid Luncheon			
Engagement Party			
Rehearsal Dinner			
Cake			
Entertainment			
Rings			
Accessories			
Other:			
Other:			
Other:			
Other:			
Other:			

Balance Due	Due Date	Over/Under Budget

Chapter Two:
Insuring your Special Day

It has been suggested that the best way to protect you from fraud is to not pay for services in full before the wedding. People have failed to realize that this is the same way vendors protect themselves. Vendors protect themselves by asking for payment in full before the wedding. This will insure that they will get paid. So, the best way to protect you is with insurance. In life you insure your vacations, home, cars, and jewelry. Why not insure one of the most important days of your life? Many companies offer wedding insurance to assist you in making sure your event is a success without loosing money. This insurance is very minimal in cost but will cover you if a vendor does not show for the wedding. Insurance is one of the important decisions you will make regarding your wedding. You want to make the right choice.

Research online companies that offer event insurance. Get a minimum of three quotes and compare the insurance plans for what will work for your special day. Visit the appendix for insurance resources.

Insurance Quote

Company	Amount Coverage	Deductible	Notes

Tip: Remember that each event would need to be insured separately if necessary. You would need to add a addendum or rider for the bridal shower, engagement party, and/or rehearsal dinner. You must consider addendums if these events will be necessary to cover.

Chapter Three:
Why Hire a Wedding Consultant?

A wedding consultant can ensure your occasion is a successful one by providing you with the essentials to plan your special day. It is important to interview a minimum of three consultants to get an understanding of there planning style and general knowledge about weddings. A good consultant can prevent you from making costly and time-consuming mistakes by advising you on etiquette, budget, and vendor selection. Consultants can give you an idea of how much things cost in the wedding industry and can lead you in the right direction with the budget you have.

You need a professional who knows the business and works with your best interest in mind. A good consultant works behind the scenes to ensure your event is a success. A good consultant provides budget analysis as well contract negotiations. A consultant is a necessity for any wedding no matter the size.

The following sheets will assist you in interviewing wedding consultants. If you need additional assistance finding a consultant in your area national associations can assist you. Consultants that belong to associations follow an ethical code. You can contact the Association of Bridal Consultants, Association of Wedding Professionals International, and International Special Events Society for assistance in finding a professional in your area. Visit the appendix for website listings.

Tip: If you don't think a coordinator is in your budget hire one for the day. To take the stress off of you. Most coordinators provide day of services.

Wedding Consultant Interview Questions

First you should find out if the initial consultation is free and if so, these questions should be asked in person. This way you can see the person and analyze their personality. You want to look at how organized the coordinator is. Look at their office and belongings to see if they keep things nice, neat, and organized. You want to choose a coordinator whose personality is similar to yours. You want to choose a person who is firm but a people person as well.

1. How long have you been in the wedding industry?
2. What is your education/experience?
3. What associations to you belong to?
4. What is your educational background?
5. How do you keep up with changes in the industry?
6. Is this your primary business?
7. What primary services do you offer?
8. What auxiliary service do you offer?
9. Will you advise us on where to best spend our money?
10. Do you have preferred vendors and do they give you discounts?
11. What items or services will you not offer?
12. Do you act as a mediator between family members?
13. Can you advise us of etiquette?
14. Are you the individual I deal with on all circumstances?
15. Do you have references I can view?
16. How do you charge for your services?
17. Do you require a deposit or retainer?
18. Will you ensure that all vendors are coordinated and on time?
19. Will you negotiate with vendors we have already selected?
20. What role will you play on the wedding day?
21. Do you have experience planning the style wedding we envision?

Interview Assessment

Interview One

Interview Date	
Consultant Name	
Company Name	
Phone Number	
Deposit Required	

Rate each consultant on a scale of one to ten in the following areas.

Topics	#	Notes
Experience		
Personality		
Creativity		
Knowledge		
Education		
References		

Interview Assessment

Interview Two

Interview Date	
Consultant Name	
Company Name	
Phone Number	
Deposit Required	

Rate each consultant on a scale of one to ten in the following areas.

Topics	#	Notes
Experience		
Personality		
Creativity		
Knowledge		
Education		
References		

Interview Assessment

Interview Three

Interview Date	
Consultant Name	
Company Name	
Phone Number	
Deposit Required	

Rate each consultant on a scale of one to ten in the following areas.

Topics	#	Notes
Experience		
Personality		
Creativity		
Knowledge		
Education		
References		

Chapter Four:
The Ceremony

In order to plan the ceremony of your dreams you must first select a site. Choosing your ceremony site can be as easy as a family church or a near by historical site perfect for outdoor ceremonies. There are several things you should consider when planning your ceremony. You should consider the weather. Weather can play a major role in the success of your special day so outdoor weddings should take place in seasons with optimal weather and a low chance of rain or storm. However, you should have a weather plan.

Before making a deposit to secure the location of your choice ask for the rules. Churches have many rules and they vary by church. Some churches don't allow secular music or flash photography during the ceremony. So, it's important to inquire about the rules of the church. If you are having an outdoors wedding ask if they have any rules on aisle runners. You may also want to ask them if they have an indoor option if the weather turns unfavorable.

Tip: It is important to communicate with the church coordinator and minister how you vision your ceremony.

You should also meet with the minister before the rehearsal to discuss how you want your ceremony to flow. At this meeting you would let the minister know if you plan to say your own vows, if you will have a reader, if you will have a soloist, or anything else special you would like to have during the ceremony that the minister needs to be aware of. You should also ask him if he attends the rehearsal and if there are any important things you should know before the wedding.

Once you have all the rules of the ceremony site remember to advise all vendors and the entire wedding party of the rules. This will ensure that everyone adheres to the rules and doesn't disrespect the ceremony site in anyway.

> *Tip: Any verbal agreements between you and the location of your choice should be given in writing. Never accept a verbal agreement always ask them to write it down or put it in an email.*

My Ceremony

Location Address: Phone:	
Contact Person:	
Church Coordinator:	
Minister:	
Number of Counseling Sessions if applicable?	
Are dressing rooms provided? If so, what time?	
Ceremony Time	
Rules for Photographer/ Video professional	
Décor Rules	
What time are you required to be out of the facility?	

Chapter Five:
The Reception

When choosing a reception venue, it is important to consider the number of guest that will be attending the wedding. Venues will sell you the space but if the size is too small or too large you may run into problems. You must consider the maximum number of individuals that could attend even if you don't expect them. The venue will need to be flexible. Most venues require you to meet a minimum amount on food and beverage for weekend weddings but will accept the final count two weeks prior. You may also want to consider having your wedding at a hotel if 50%-60% of guests are traveling from out of state. Hotels will give you great room block rates and you can negotiate getting a suite for the night at no charge due to having your wedding at the hotel. No matter what venue you choose, it is important to do your research and consider your guests.

You should visit and interview at least two venues. Use the pages to follow as a guide to the questions you should ask and the responses received from each venue.

Tip: Don't be afraid to question anything you don't understand or agree with in the contract. If there is something you don't agree with let them know you will not sign it unless they allow you to cross it out. If you do cross it out have a representative initial the section.

Interview One

Do you provide catering services?	
Do you have a liquor license?	
Do you have a wedding package that includes all of your services?	
Is cake cutting included in the package?	
Pricing per person?	
Is the bar included in the package?	
What are your bar options?	
Is valet parking included the package?	
What is the maximum number of people that can be held in the banquet room?	
What is the weekend minimum?	
Is there a room rental fee?	
What is the gratuity percentage?	
What are the rules for the banquet room?	
Is there an extra fee for a cocktail hour?	
What time can my vendors arrive?	
Does your table linen go to the floor?	
Do you have skirting available for all your tables?	

Interview Two

Do you provide catering services?	
Do you have a liquor license?	
Do you have a wedding package that includes all of your services?	
Is cake cutting included in the package?	
Pricing per person?	
Is the bar included in the package?	
What are your bar options?	
Is valet parking included the package?	
What is the maximum number of people that can be held in the banquet room?	
What is the weekend minimum?	
Is there a room rental fee?	
What is the gratuity percentage?	
What are the rules for the banquet room?	
Is there an extra fee for a cocktail hour?	
What time can my vendors arrive?	
Does your table linen go to the floor?	
Do you have skirting available for all your tables?	

If the venue you chose does not provide catering or alcohol you will have to hire a caterer. Research caterers that are capable of providing all the service you need to make your day perfect. It will be easier to handle one vendor to provide both food and beverage. Use the pages to follow as a guide to interviewing possible caterer and recording there responses.

Interview One

Do you hold a license to cater?	
Do you hold a liquor license?	
Do you have set packages to choose from?	
Can you accommodate special menu requests?	
How many servers will be provided?	
How many bartenders will be provided?	
Do you provide bar equipment?	
Will you prepare the food onsite or will it be ready to serve?	
How will you keep the food warm?	
Do you provide the eating utensils (i.e. china and silverware)?	

Interview Two

Do you hold a license to cater?	
Do you hold a liquor license?	
Do you have set packages to choose from?	
Can you accommodate special menu requests?	
How many servers will be provided?	
How many bartenders will be provided?	
Do you provide bar equipment?	
Will you prepare the food onsite or will it be ready to serve?	
How will you keep the food warm?	
Do you provide the eating utensils (i.e. china and silverware)?	

My Reception

Location Address: Phone:	
Contact Person:	
Banquet Manager:	
Cocktail Hour Start Time	
Reception Start Time	
Time dinner is served	
Time of cake cutting	
End Time	

My Reception Vendors

Wedding Coordinator	
Florist	
Baker	
Decorator	
Ice Sculpture	
Chocolate Fountain	
Entertainment	
Video professional	
Photographer	
Caterer	

Notes:

Chapter Six:
Choosing Your Wedding Cake

Today there are many styles and flavors to choose from when selecting wedding cakes. Choosing a cake will be a difficult task but research is important. Wedding magazines feature many different cake styles and will be your number one guide to finding your dream cake.

You should begin searching for a pastry chef six to eight months before your wedding date. This will allow you the opportunity of reserving your date with the pastry chef of choice without any hassles. You should begin by looking at different cake styles to get an idea of the shape you would like prior to contacting the chef.

You should also discuss with your groom whether or not he wants a groom's cake. The groom's cake is a southern tradition and is usually chocolate. Many southerners reserve this tradition but it is becoming more common. Groom's cakes are unique to the taste and interests of the groom, and is ultimately his choice.

With all this in mind you should now begin to contact pastry chefs and schedule appointments for taste testing. You want to let them know what your interests are whether it is in just a wedding cake or both a wedding and groom's cake. It is important to let the baker know the flavors you are interested in tasting. The cake tasting should be complimentary to the bride and groom. You should not make more than two appointments. It is okay to make more appointments if you have decided not to go with your first two choices. However, do your research? Family and friends are a great resource to use. Your consultant can also help you in this area.

Pastry Chef Interview Questions

1. Do you have pictures of previous designs?
2. How long have you done wedding cakes?
3. Are there extra charges associated with your cakes?
4. Will you decorate the cake with fresh or silk flowers?
5. How far in advance are your cakes prepared?
6. Do you charge a fee for delivery?
7. How much do you charge per slice for a wedding and/or groom's cake?

Interview One

Name	
Phone	
Price	
Delivery	
Deposit Required	
Flavors Tasted	
Notes	

Interview Two

Name	
Phone	
Price	
Delivery	
Deposit Required	
Flavors Tasted	
Notes	

My Wedding Cake

Pastry Chef	
Phone	
Deposit	
Balance Due Date	
Order Date	

Wedding Cake

Number to Serve	
Shape	
Flavor	
Filling Flavor	
Icing Color/Flavor	
Decoration	
Topper	
Description	

Grooms Cake

Number to Serve	
Shape	
Flavor	
Filling Flavor	
Icing Color/Flavor	
Decoration	
Description	

Chapter Seven:
Choosing Your Bridal Party

Choosing your bridal party can be a difficult task. It is important to extend the invitation and allow the potential attendants to accept or decline the invitation. Being a attendant is a very important and time consuming task. Individuals have to be prepared both financially and time wise to make a commitment. There are several things you should consider when inviting someone to play a role in the wedding. You should be very honest with them regarding what type of commitment this would be. It is important to understand if a person declines the role. They may be able to assist in other areas but not prepared to make the commitment you have asked them to.

When inviting individuals to be a part of your bridal party. It is important to invite people to play roles that are compatible to there personalities. You should ask yourself the following questions.

1. Are they reliable?
2. Can they financially handle the requirements?
3. Is there personality suitable for the role you have chosen them to play?

For example when choosing a greeter you should look for an outgoing people person. This person should be helpful and willing to assist you in making your guests feel welcomed. When choosing hostesses or ushers you should look for those individuals whom are responsible and helpful. These individuals would assist in seating guests and transferring gifts from ceremony to reception if needed. When choosing a maid of honor you should choose someone whom is close to you, responsible and organized. They are responsible for assisting throughout the planning process as well as organizing the bridal shower.

Use the attached attendant role as a guide to what each person in the wedding party is responsible for. Remember the average wedding has at least four bridesmaids, four groomsmen, one flower girl, one ringer bearer, two ushers, and two hostesses.

Tip: Remember to thank your attendants for sharing a role in your special day. Make them feel appreciated and important. Welcome gifts and personalized thank you notes are just one way to accomplish this task.

Potential Wedding Party Contact

Use this form to list the contact information of those you have extended an invitation to.

Name	Role	Phone #	Contact Date	Accept/ Decline Invitation

My Wedding Party

Use this form to list the contact information of those whom have accepted your invitation.

Name	Role	Phone #	Cell #	Address	Email

Attendant Roles

Matron of Honor- Usually a close friend or sister, whom is married, stands by the bride during the ceremony and assists the bride by holding her bouquet and keeping the brides train straightened. The matron stands at the head of the line formation. She/he is also responsible for assisting the bride through the planning as well as throwing the bridal shower and/or bachelorette party. She/he is also responsible for toasting the bride and groom at reception.

Maid of Honor- Usually is a close friend or sister. She/he stands behind the Matron (if no matron she stands at the head of the line formation and performs matron and maid duties). She assists the bride with her train by making sure that it is straight during the ceremony. She/he is also responsible for throwing the bridal shower and/or bachelorette party. She/ He is also responsible for toasting the bride and groom at reception.

Best Man- Usually is the best friend or brother of the groom. He stands at the right of the groom carrying the ring. He is also responsible for toasting the bride and groom as well, as throwing the bachelor party.

Bridesmaid- traditionally is there to support the bride. Generally couples have between one and eight bridesmaids. They assist the bride when needed and help to make her comfortable while she waits for the ceremony to begin. They may also play a role in the giving of the bridal shower.

Junior Bridesmaids- are children who are too young to be a bridesmaid but too old to be a flower girl. They generally walk down the aisle unaccompanied or with a junior groomsman.

Groomsmen- Like bridesmaids, groomsmen traditionally lend support to the groom. This can be close friends and family members. They may also play a role in the bachelor party.

Flower Girl- Follows down the aisle behind the bridesmaids and throw rose petals down for the bride. They are generally between the ages three and five.
Younger children may walk down in pairs.

Ring Bearer- The ring bearer carries a pillow with the wedding rings attached but fake rings may be used. The ring bearer should be comfortable in front of an audience.

Ushers- seats guests and parents of bride and groom as well as lay down the aisle runner for bride. This role will be further assigned at the ceremony.

Hostess- greets guest, passes out program, and shows guest where the restrooms are located. Hostess also assists coordinator when needed.

Guest book attendant/ hostess- greet all guests with excitement and enthusiasm, ask guests to sign guest book and follow usher to sit. Also sets aside any gifts given to the couple.

Chapter Eight:
Bridal Attire

Choosing the Perfect Wedding Dress

Choosing a wedding dress can be a very difficult task. Before starting your search you should find out what you like and don't like. Magazines are helpful in helping you do this. Look through bridal magazines or online to find dresses you like. Cut out the pictures and take them with you to bridal shops. This will give the consultant an idea of your taste and style. You should also know the different type of wedding dress silhouettes.

- ❖ Ball Gown- The ball gown is designed with a fitted bodice, which gives a slimming effect on the waist. It is paired with a very full skirt that begins at the bride's natural waistline.

- ❖ Sheath- The sheath is meant to hug the body, embracing all the curves of the bride. It is a straight length dress.

- ❖ A-line- The A-line design is ideal for almost any body type. It features a fitted bodice and a slight flair that begins at the waistline and cascades to the floor.

- ❖ Mermaid- The mermaid design is meant to hug the natural curves of the bride. It also has a flair that begins at the knees.

Once you are familiar with the silhouettes above you can begin to figure out which style compliments your figure.

Don't buy the first dress you find. Once you have found the one you want check with other stores to get the best pricing and service. Use the chart attached to list the stores and the style number of the dress you love.

Negotiate with the store regarding alterations. See if you can get a flat rate or a cap on the alterations. This will insure that no matter how many alterations you need the, amount won't exceed what you have budgeted. Private dress shops are more willing to negotiate on pricing than chain retail shops.

> *Tip: Don't be afraid to asking the consultant for gown suggestions based on your figure. They are the experts and should know what silhouette will best fit your shape.*

My Wedding Dress

Style #	Designer	Store Name	Price

First Fitting Appointment:
Alterations Appointment:
Final Fitting Appointment:

Choosing Wedding Party Attire

Selecting attire for your wedding party can be a difficult task. It is important to think of the individuals wearing the clothing when making a selection. When choosing bridesmaids attire look for attire that will compliment the shape of your bridesmaids. Many designers are creating a line called "separates", which can be mixed and matched to fit different shapes but are created in the same colors. This is really easy for bridesmaids and allows them to have some insight into what they are wearing. As the bride you can match up several styles and give your bridesmaids choices.

Most dress boutiques will give you a discount on your bridesmaids dress for placing your dress order and the bridesmaid dress order with them. It is important that if a discount is not offered you negotiate one if you plan to utilize the store for your dress and the bridesmaid's dresses.

> *Tip: When choosing a dress be sure to ask what sizes the dress is available in. This will insure that they have a size available for everyone in your bridal party. Also ask for any additional fees for sizes over a twelve.*

Groomsmen are not as difficult as bridesmaids but it is imperative to have a swatch from the bridesmaids dress in order to match the tuxedo accessories. If the groomsmen are traveling from out-of-state it is essential that they come in town early enough to have a tuxedo fitting and allow time for corrections to be made. Sometimes measurements get lost in translation and a final fitting is important. Most tuxedo companies offer a free grooms tuxedo rental with a certain number of paid rentals. They also offer discounts on young children tuxedos. As you decide which company to use, ask them about their specials. You should also ask them how long it takes to make changes to a tuxedo order.

Use the attached charts to keep track of the attire you choose for your wedding party and your appointments.

> *Tip: When choosing tuxedos choose a style that best fits your wedding. Be conscious of the time of day and the bridesmaid's dresses. If the bridesmaids dress is a formal ball gown you want to go with a formal black tuxedo.*

Bridesmaid Dresses

Style #	Designer	Deposit Required	Price

Fitting Appointment:
Alterations Appointment:
Final Fitting Appointment:

Store Name & Number:
Contact Person:

Tuxedo

Grooms Party	Style	Colors	Price
Groomsmen			
Groom			
Usher			
Ringbearer			

Final Fitting Appointment:

Store Name & Number:

Contact Person:

Chapter Nine:
Choosing a Photographer

When choosing a photographer it is important to know the different styles of shooting. There are two types of shooting styles photojournalistic and traditional. The difference between the two is photojournalist take more natural and fun photos. Their photos are usually not posed and you don't even notice their presence throughout the day. They also take intimate, small detail photographs that sort of tell a story. These photographers pricing are usually more expensive than traditional photographers. This is the most popular style of photography and many brides are choosing to go with these photographers. Traditional photographers have been around since the beginning. They take classic photographs that are usually posed or staged. If they miss something during the ceremony they will stage it again for a picture. If you are looking for classic photographs traditional photographers are the best at doing this. Their pricing is usually less expensive than photojournalist but it depends on the packages you choose. Most photographers offer black and white photos as part of their services.

You must also consider the type of media they utilize for taking pictures. Do they use film or digital? Film is becoming obsolete. Photographers are being forced to move into the age of computers because companies are no longer making cameras that utilize film. Digital photography is the most popular and brides prefer it to film because of the editing features. Digital photography is much easier to edit. Blemishes, marks, and color can be changed fairly easily.

You should interview a minimum of two photographers before making a decision on whom to go with. When interviewing use the graph on the following page for questions to ask and to record the vendor's answers.

Interview One

What style of photography do you utilize?	
How many years have you been in business?	
How much of your business is weddings?	
Do you have references?	
Do you utilize Film or Digital equipment?	
Do you charge extra for multiple locations?	
Is there an extra charge for black and white photos?	
Are we required to feed the staff?	
How much is charged for overtime?	
Do we have to purchase our proofs separately?	
Are engagement photos included in your packages?	
Are these fees for filming the rehearsal dinner or bridal shower?	
How long will it take for the pictures to be completed?	
Do you offer editing and if so, is there a fee?	
Do you offer a signing board and frame?	

Interview Two

What style of photography do you utilize?	
How many years have you been in business?	
How much of your business is weddings?	
Do you have references?	
Do you utilize Film or Digital equipment?	
Do you charge extra for multiple locations?	
Is there an extra charge for black and white photos?	
Are we required to feed the staff?	
How much is charged for overtime?	
Do we have to purchase our proofs separately?	
Are engagement photos included in your packages?	
Are these fees for filming the rehearsal dinner or bridal shower?	
How long will it take for the pictures to be completed?	
Do you offer editing and if so, is there a fee?	
Do you offer a signing board and frame?	

Once you have made the final decision use this space to record contact information and information on your selected package.

Chapter Ten:
Choosing Your Video Professional

Like photographers, video professional have different artistic styles. Journalistic and documentary is the most common for wedding video professional. Journalistic style tells a story and paints a picture of the wedding through video. Documentary style shows the event exactly has it happens. Both styles use introductions and transitions to jazz up the presentation. It is up to you to decide exactly what style you like best. In order to understand the difference between the two it is important to see the professionals completed work. Ask for a sample to take with you if possible. This will help you decide if you like the professional's artistic style.

Cinematography is the latest artistic style in capturing memories. This unique style is utilized to capture big screen movies. Because of the utilization of tradition movie film and equipment brides love it. It is like starring in your own made for big screen movie. Cinematography is much more expensive than video starting at $20,000. If your budget allows and you want the best method of capturing memories cinematography is the way to go.

Once you have decided what style will fit into your budget. You should interview no less than two industry professionals. This will assist you in comparing their work and making an informed decision. Use the attached interview questions as a guide to finding the best and most qualified company for you.

Interview One

What style of video do you specialize?	
How many years have you been in business?	
How much of your business is weddings?	
Do you have references?	
Do you charge extra for multiple locations?	
Is there an extra charge for two video professional filming the wedding?	
Are we required to feed the staff?	
How much is charged for overtime?	
How long do you keep the raw footage?	
Is the raw footage available for purchase?	
What are the fees for filming the rehearsal dinner or bridal shower?	
How long will it take for the video to be completed?	
Can we select our own music?	
Is a photomontage included in the video?	
If we don't like a portion of the video can that portion be edited out?	
Are we given the opportunity to approve the video before it is completed?	

Interview Two

What style of video do you specialize?	
How many years have you been in business?	
How much of your business is weddings?	
Do you have references?	
Do you charge extra for multiple locations?	
Is there an extra charge for two video professional filming the wedding?	
Are we required to feed the staff?	
How much is charged for overtime?	
How long do you keep the raw footage?	
Is the raw footage available for purchase?	
Fees for filming the rehearsal dinner or bridal shower?	
How long will it take for the video to be complete?	
Can we select our own music?	
Is a photomontage included in the video?	
If we don't like a portion of the video can that portion be edited?	
Are we given the opportunity to approve the video before it is completed?	

My Wedding Video Professional

Company Name	
Company Address	
Company Phone	
Contact Person	
Hours of Coverage	
Guarantee	
Refund/Cancellation Policy	
Payment Options	
Deposit	
Balance Due and Date	

Chapter Eleven:
Stationery

Save the Date Cards

Save the date cards are important to allow your guests enough notice to prepare to attend your wedding. If they are out of state they will need to make travel arrangements and these cards give them the date in order to begin making arrangements. Save the dates should be sent out six months to one year before the wedding. If you are having a destination wedding save the date cards should be sent out as soon as a date and location has been finalized.

Invitations

The most confusing part of ordering invitations is what should be included in the invitation. You should include the invitation, reception card, response card, and direction card. These are all very important in knowing that your guest will arrive to the wedding. In some cultures gift registry notices are also included.

In order to place your order you will have to make several decisions. You need to decide on wording. It is tradition to include parent's names if they are paying for the wedding. Discuss the wording with your family before placing the order. Making changes to your order after the order is placed will prolong the order. You will also have to decide on the ink color, type style, and lined envelope color (optional) to place the order.

It is proper etiquette to send invitations to your wedding party. It is also appropriate to invite the minister and his/her spouse. You should order a minimum twenty-five extra invitations to ensure that you don't run out. All invitations should include a return address that can be utilized by guests if they would like to send gifts or a personal note.

Postage is a major consideration with invitations. It is best to take one to the post office to be weighed. Additional postage maybe required for oddly shaped invitations so it is important to take one in for accurate pricing.

Additional Stationery

After placing the invitation order you will need to consider place cards, wedding programs, and thank you notes. These items will complete your stationery responsibilities. All of these items are needed make sure your wedding day runs smoothly. Separate thank you notes should be sent for shower gifts and wedding gifts.

Use the enclosed planning chart to stay on top of deadlines and what should be ordered.

My Wedding Stationary

Item	Quantity	Item Number	Typestyle
Save the Dates			
Invitations			
Response			
Reception Card			
Thank you Notes			
Place Card			
Programs			

Tip: It is important to order proofs for all stationary orders. This will ensure accuracy of order. There is nominal fee for proofs. This service can save you from making costly mistakes.

Ink Color	Pricing	Deadline Date

Company Name	
Company Address	
Company Phone	
Date Order Placed	
Delivery Date	

Chapter Twelve
Wedding Décor

You may ask what is décor. Décor is the arrangement of decorations utilized to make your special day unique. It can range from fine china to linen. Your decorum is an important aspect to consider when planning a wedding. There are many things that can enhance your special day. Linen, props, lighting, and flowers are the most common items utilized to enhance décor.

> Tip: When thinking of décor consider what is the most important to you and your guests and focus your attention in that area.

Lighting

Event lighting companies can add to the ambiance and mood of your event by adding color through lighting. They can put emphasis on certain areas through spot lighting. You can enhance your day by having your names projected on the floor or by having strolling lights through out the room. These are just a few ways lighting can enhance your event. They can also illuminate your centerpieces with colored lighting. Event lighting companies design packages based on your visions and budget. Lighting can begin at $500 and go up from there based on your design. Before securing a lighting vendor ask to see their work, events that they have done. Don't be afraid to ask questions. They will try to sell you more than what you need be sure to tell them exactly what you like and obtain quotes on that design. Obtain no less than two quotes and no more than three. You always want to compare design and pricing.

Quote 1

Company	
Price	
Quality of Design	

Quote 2

Company	
Price	
Quality of Design	

Quote 3

Company	
Price	
Quality of Design	

Tip: Before finalizing your lighting find out if the venue will allow you to use there electrical outlets or will you need to add a generator in the budget. There should be a meeting that involves you, the lighting company, and venue.

Linen

Linen can be used in many ways to enhance your day. No matter what the budget linen even in the smallest details can be utilized. Chair covers are the most popular form of linen used. They are available in many designs from full back to sheer. They are also available in various sizes and are designed to fit most any chair. Chair covers can make your event very elegant by themselves. So, if you have a small budget a basic chair cover may give you the look you want. Utilize the Internet and magazines to get an idea of how chair covers look and what style you like. When choosing a chair cover there are several questions to be asked so use the chart below to fill in your answers. This chart will assist you in letting the linen company know what you are looking for.

Chair style	
Indoor or Outdoor Usage	
Approximately How Many Are Needed	
Sash or No Sash	
Fabric of Sash	
Style of Chair Cover/Fabric of Chair Cover	

Table Cloths may or may not fit into your budget however small accents of tablecloths can enhance any room. Tablecloths can be used on the cake table to make it stand out or to accent the head table. Tablecloths come in many sizes, lengths, and designs. You must decide if you want a floor length look or the look of an overlay. Table runners can also be used instead of tablecloths to add a splash of color to the table. The chart below will assist you in deciding what will work best for you special day.

Table Cloths or Runners	
Size of Table	
Floor Length or Drape	
Approx. Number of Tables	
Will they be utilized on head table	
Colors Needed	
Swatch Styles Interested In Viewing	

Linen Quote

Company	
Price	
Installation Fee	

Tip: Ask the company of your choice for samples. Most companies will allow you to take the samples to the venue to ensure that you have the look you want.

My Linen Rental Company

Company Name	
Address	
Contact Person and Phone #	

Prop Rental

What is the purpose of prop rental? Well, many brides have a vision of how they want there wedding to be and in order to achieve that vision it is important to rent décor items. For example, if any of your guests enjoy cigars you may decide to have a cigar lounge. Lounge furniture would be a key feature of a cigar lounge. Prop rental companies rent many different items from statues to furniture. They also provide draping, china, and much more. So if you have a vision in mind but don't know how to achieve it, a prop house may be able to assist you with your rental needs. Before contacting a prop house you should have an idea of exactly what it is you want to rent. A visit to the prop house maybe necessary to get an idea of what they an offer you. Answer the questions below. Then utilize the chart to list the items you are interested in renting and tracking the cost of the rentals.

What is your vision?
What do you need to accomplish this vision?

Item	Quote 1	Quote 2

Tip: When renting props it is important to ask the dimensions of the prop to ensure the proper fit.

My Prop Rental Company

Company Name	
Address	
Contact Person and Phone #	

Floral Décor

There are two types of florist retail and event. Retail florists are those you see driving down the street. They not only service events but also sell individual arrangements through FTD and walk in clients. Many of them have a catalog that they allow their brides to look through and pick out arrangements. Event florists usual do not own a store. Instead they work out of a design studio. Event florists specialize in social and corporate events of any size. Event florist are creative and typically come up with unique ideas. Event florists usually stay until your wedding party is pinned and have received all their flowers. It is important that before deciding on which florist to utilize, you compare the work of an event florist to the work of a retail florist. Once you have made a decision, make sure they have your vision in mind. Use the comparison chart to keep track of your interviews.

Before interviewing a florist you should know what your basic needs are. Use the chart below as a guide.

# Bridesmaids bouquets	
# Groomsmen boutonnières	
Mother Corsages	
Father Boutonnieres	
Usher Boutonnieres	
Hostess Corsages	
Flower girl	
Ring bearer	
Grandmother	
Grandfather	
Memorial Arrangements	
Miscellaneous Flowers	

Tip: When choosing your flowers try to choose flowers that are in season. Flowers that are out of season will be more costly than in season flowers.

Interview 1

Company Name	
Type of Florist	
How long have you been in business?	
Are you limited to the work shown in your album?	
Do you stay and pin the wedding party?	
What are your delivery and setup fees?	
Can you give me a quote of the flowers we discussed before I make a decision?	
Can I make changes to the order after the contract has been signed?	
How many weddings do you service a year?	

Interview 2

Company Name	
Type of Florist	
How long have you been in business?	
Are you limited to the work shown in your album?	
Do you stay and pin the wedding party?	
What are your delivery and setup fees?	
Can you give me a quote of the flowers we discussed before I make a decision?	
Can I make changes to the order after the contract has been signed?	
How many weddings do you service a year?	

My Wedding Florist

Company Name	
Address	
Contact Person and Phone #	

Chapter Thirteen:
Entertainment

Choosing the right entertainment can be difficult. You should think of your guests and the theme of your wedding when choosing entertainment. Entertainment can be in the form of a dance troop, a skit, band, and/or disc jockey. The genre or type of music should also be considered. If you have a very diverse group of guest you may want to hire a diverse band or disc jockey, maybe even two disc jockeys or bands to cover the type of music you are looking for. Research is very important. Entertainment companies or disk jockey services can assist you in obtaining your entertainment goals. For instance, if you are having a Spanish themed wedding you should consider Mariachi band or Flamingo dancer. Entertainment can ensure that your guests have a great time. Don't be afraid to try something new. Ask for demos of the group or to meet with the manager. Use the chart below to rate the groups. You should look into more than one group in each area of interest.

Questions you should consider:
What type of music?
How long do you need them to perform?

Questions to ask the company:
How long have you been in business?
Will you act as the master of ceremonies?
Are you familiar with wedding protocol?

Be sure to review all contracts for information on breaks, gratuities, and overtime. Use the chart below to compare quotes. Record your final decisions in the section titled "My Wedding Entertainment".

Company	Genre	Pricing	#of Breaks

Gratuities	Overtime Pricing	Guarantee

My Wedding Entertainment

Company Name	
Company Location	
Company Phone/Contact Person	
Hours of Service	
Start Time/End time	

Company Name	
Company Location	
Company Phone/Contact Person	
Hours of Service	
Start Time/End time	

Company Name	
Company Location	
Company Phone/Contact Person	
Hours of Service	
Start Time/End time	

Company Name	
Company Location	
Company Phone/Contact Person	
Hours of Service	
Start Time/End time	

Company Name	
Company Location	
Company Phone/Contact Person	
Hours of Service	
Start Time/End time	

Tip: It is important to allow your entertainment the opportunity to take breaks and touch basis with the planner.

Chapter Fourteen:
Rehearsal

The rehearsal is important to the success of the wedding. Everyone involved in the wedding should be at the rehearsal to know his or her role. This includes parents of the bride, parents of the groom, grandparents, bridesmaids, groomsmen, ushers, hostesses, flower girls, ring bearer, readers, soloist, and the minister(if he/she is available). A rehearsal should be no longer than one hour in length but can expand to two hours for those who are late. It is also important that someone professional conduct the rehearsal. This will ensure that things happen according to proper etiquette. In many traditions it is considered bad luck if the bride plays herself in the rehearsal so, it is important that the bride select a replacement for the rehearsal if she believes in this superstition. The bride must be there even if she is not participating in the rehearsal itself. At the rehearsal there should be a run through of the entire ceremony once without music while everyone is getting acquainted with his or her role in the wedding and once with music. It is the responsibility of the coordinator to show people where to stand.

The receiving line is optional. Many brides are doing with out the receiving line and replacing this with a cocktail hour or something more festive. However the receiving can be done at the church or reception hall. The church is the most popular location. Spacing and the size of the line will need to be considered when making a decision on the receiving line, is a tradition of the wedding party lining up to great guests.

My Wedding Rehearsal

Location	
Date	
Time	

Tip: Tell your bridal party To be at the rehearsal thirty minutes before the scheduled start time. This will ensure the rehearsal starts and ends on time.

It is proper etiquette to host a rehearsal dinner. Rehearsal dinners are to thank your family and friends for sharing a part in your special day. The dinner is usually after rehearsal but if you are having a late rehearsal the dinner can be before the rehearsal or in the form of a luncheon. Restaurants are great places for rehearsal dinners and are usually prepared to host such an event. Many restaurants have special menu pricing and private dining rooms to encourage parties. If you are hosting your reception at a hotel they may offer you a 10%-15% discount on hosting your rehearsal dinner in the hotels restaurant. Rehearsal dinners are usually hosted by the groom's family and can be held at the family's home. It is important to find out before the rehearsal dinner who will be paying for it and plan accordingly.

My Rehearsal Dinner

Location Name and Address	
Date and Time	
Contact Person and Phone #	

Chapter Fifthteen:
Transportation

Choosing the right transportation is complicated. You have to ask yourself "will you be transporting the entire wedding party". If so, you have to decide where they would leave their vehicles and how they will be transported. Many couples have gotten away from renting party buses all though they are fun they are not very stylish. Most common ways to stylishly transport an entire wedding party is renting stretch hummers, navigators, or expeditions. These vehicles hold between 18-26 individuals and would accommodate large wedding parties.

Antique limos like Rolls Royce and Jaguars are more popular for the bride and groom. But if you like fairytales a horse and carriage can do the job.

The most important thing to look for in a limo contract is there guarantee or back up plan. What will they do if the vehicle breaks down? Will they give you a complete refund? Are they being held accountable? Some transportation companies take advantage of their clients by putting clauses in small print that says that they are not responsible if the limo breaks down. Be aware of this and do not reserve a company who cannot guarantee their service.

> *Tip: Be sure to read the small print in your transportation contract. You should make sure that they will guarantee you transportation if the vehicle you reserved malfunctions.*

Company	Type of Vehicle	# Of vehicles	Guarantee

# of Hours	Pricing	Gratuity

My Transportation Company

Company Name	
Address	
Contact Person and Phone #	
Vehicle Reserved	

Chapter Sixteen:
Reserving Your Honeymoon

Finding a great place to go on your honeymoon isn't difficult at all. There are cruises and resorts that would be absolutely beautiful and a great place to spend your honeymoon. Travel Agents play a key role in assisting you in planning your dream honeymoon. Travel Agents have a fee that is usually include in the price of your travel package. You should work with an agent that specializes in weddings and honeymoons. In order to specialize in honeymoons they have traveled the locations and explored the surroundings. Many of them have received certifications on there knowledge of the resorts. They can tell you what sites to see and what tours to avoid. Many of these companies advertise online.

If you are considering planning the honeymoon yourself be careful. The pictures online are not always what you get. If considering this option you may want to travel to a place you are familiar with and make sure you obtain travel insurance. You would hate to have a horrible memory of your honeymoon. So, consider using a travel agent.

You should consider several things before reserving your honeymoon. First, do you need a passport and if so, do you have enough time to obtain one before your travel dates. You also need to know your travel dates before contacting an agent. You may also consider obtaining travel insurance this will just insure that you are covered against lost baggage and theft on your honeymoon.

The "Bridal Guide" has an online honeymoon-planning page on their site. Visit them online at _www.bridalguide. com_.

Want to travel to the Bahamas for your honeymoon try _www.nassauparadiseisland.com_

Other Reference Sites:

www.eliteislands.com
www.francevacations.com
www.bulafijinow.com
www.newmexico.org
www.dreambrides.com
www.visitbarbados.com
www.rexresorts.com
www.bg.visitflorida.com
www.visitmybeach.com

Enter Quotes Below

Destination	# of Days	Accommodations

Airline	Agent	Pricing

My Honeymoon Arrangements

Dates of Travel:	
Airline:	
Time of Departure:	
Hotel:	
Transportation from airport to hotel:	
Is passport needed:	
Agent Information:	

Chapter Seventeen:
Your Wedding Day

This chapter is designed to inform you of what you need to ensure your day runs smoothly. All vendors should be confirmed one week prior to wedding. Some vendors will require final detailing appointments. During this appointment, it is imperative that you confirm the arrival times and exit time. You should also go over what the vendor is responsible for in detail.

You should send the bridal party a detailed itinerary of all wedding related activities. The itinerary should include arrival times and locations. You may want to also include directions. This information should be given to the bridal party twice once by mail and again upon arrival to the rehearsal. Some members of the bridal party may loose or forget there itinerary so, have extra copies available.

So, it's your wedding day and what should you do now. It's your day! You should relax and let someone else do the work. This is the day you have prepared for. It is one of the most important moments of your life. You should only be concerned with pampering yourself. So, if you have gotten to this point with out a coordinator. You should at least consider hiring one to handle the day of requirements and take the stress off yourself. But if you have not hired one you need to assign someone to be responsible for confirming the vendors and greeting them as they arrive. You also need someone to be responsible for making sure your day runs as smoothly as possible. These people should not be involved in the wedding. This person or family member should be reliable and capable of handling any concerns that arise. Debrief the responsible person at least two weeks prior to the wedding to let them know what you expect from the vendors. This way if the bakery delivers the wrong cake they will know it is the wrong cake.

The day of your wedding should be relaxing. In order to ensure it is you should prepare things in advance. Take care of as much as possible the day before. For instance take your wedding dress and accessories to the ceremony site the day before. Ask them to lock your things in a secure place. This will ensure you don't forget important items. You may also want to get your nails done and get your hair set. Plan to have everything done the day before your wedding. You should also plan to have your make up and hair done onsite on your wedding day. This will keep you from worrying about traffic or waiting in a salon most of your wedding day.

Tip: Advance planning will free you from stress on the day of your wedding.

Use the chart below to list your pre-wedding day tasks.

Task 1	
Task 2	
Task 3	
Task 4	
Task 5	
Task 6	
Task 7	
Task 8	
Task 9	
Task 10	

Use the chart below to list your day of wedding appointments.

Appointment 1	
Appointment 2	
Appointment 3	
Appointment 4	
Appointment 5	

Chapter Eighteen:
Conclusion

This book was designed with you in mind. Over the years we have heard brides state that there were things in the planning process that they wish they could go back and change. Many of their concerns involved vendors. The vendor did not get their vision or did not provide the service contracted. This book was designed to guide you through the planning process so you don't have to look back and wish you had made different decisions. Carry this guide with you to your appointments and remember to use the charts to record your conversations. Refresh yourself before every vendor appointment by going through the section on their services. The first step to planning your special day is organizing your information. This book helps you to stay organized by allowing you a place to store the information.

Stay on track by following this guide chapter by chapter and noting the helpful tips. These tips were prepared based on the mistakes other brides have made. They will assist you in the things you would normally forget. At the end of the planning process you should have your dream wedding and vendors you can rely on.

Tip: Never reserve vendors on impulse Make sure that they meet your standards and budget requirements.

Appendix

Budget Resources
www.theweddingreport.com

Insurance Resources
www.wedsafe.com
www.weddinguard.com
www.protectmywedding.com

Professional Associations
www.ises.com
www.awpi.com
www.bridalassn.com

Planning Software
www.ezweddingplanner.com

Vendor Resources
www.theknot.com
www.weddingchannel.com
www.brides.com